MW00999351

The Beauty of
IRELAND

Published in Ireland by
Gill & Macmillan Ltd
Hume Avenue, Park West, Dublin 12
with associated companies throughout the world
www.gillmacmillan.ie
CLB 4653
Originally published by CLB Publishing Limited, 1996
copyright © Salamander Books Limited, 2001
A member of the Chrysalis Group plc
ISBN 0 7171 2377 4
Printed in Hong Kong
All rights reserved. No part of this publication may be copied,
reproduced or transmitted in any form or by any means without
permission of the publisher.

The Beauty of
IRELAND

Gill & Macmillan

For thousands of years, Ireland was at the edge of the known world. The island lies on the most westerly tip of the vast Eurasian landmass. To the west, there is nothing except the Atlantic Ocean. To the east there is another small island, Britain, and then beyond that the great North European plain runs away to the Ural Mountains. Beyond the Urals, Siberia folds around the curve of the world until it reaches the Bering Strait, almost touching Alaska. For most of human history, therefore, Ireland was at the very edge of the known world.

The Romans, who went just about everywhere, never bothered with Ireland. After all, everyone knew that Ireland was just an island on the edge of nowhere. Everyone, that is, except the Irish, who were certain that there was something out there beyond the ocean. They proved it, too. It is widely believed that Irishman St Brendan discovered America a thousand years before Columbus sailed.

Like St Brendan, the Irish have always been curious about the outside world. They have not always been willing emigrants, but they have been remarkably successful ones. Today, in the United States alone, forty million people are proud to claim Irish descent, and all around the world there is ample testimony to the intelligence, hard work and determination of Irish people.

Ireland is her people. But the Irish people are, in turn, formed by the magnificent combination of landscape and climate that is the island of Ireland. The country is a mixture of magnificent mountains, rolling and fertile plains and clear, unpolluted rivers and lakes. Although the Irish often complain about the weather, they are in fact blessed with one of the most benign climates in the world. There are no extremes of heat or cold, and when the sun shines, it is a paradise.

Perhaps it is this temperate and gentle climate that gives the country and the people their character. Ireland is relaxed and easy-going, not given to hurry or excess and always ready with a welcome for the stranger. *Céad mile fáilte* is the traditional Gaelic greeting: a hundred thousand welcomes. So it has always been and always will be.

So relax and enjoy the country where time goes more slowly and the people are more friendly and life is gentler than anywhere else you have ever been. See the magnificent and majestic scenery of Kerry and Cork, with Killarney – 'heaven's reflection' – at its centre. Visit rugged Connemara and, just to the north of it, the lakes of Mayo and the Yeats country. Travel the stunningly beautiful coast of Donegal, or the Glens of Antrim, two of Ireland's best kept secrets. Marvel at the rich river valleys of the southeast and the rolling, fertile fields of the Golden Vale rippling across north Munster from east Tipperary to the very borders of Kerry itself. And don't forget the towns and cities: Dublin, one of the truly great world capitals, sophisticated and yet small enough not to have lost its human dimension; Belfast, a fine Victorian city surrounded by the most gorgeous countryside; Cork, the Venice of the south; Galway, a centre of learning and the arts, with its fabled bay; Limerick, standing proudly at the head of the Shannon estuary – the list goes on.

So welcome to Ireland: *céad mile fáilte*. Ireland is no longer at the edge of the world. It is, in a strange way, the centre of the world. Or at least it is the centre of that world in which people strive to lead a good and decent life, in which human values prevail and where no one is ever too busy to throw you a wave or a greeting. Enjoy it, and when your visit ends you will discover, like so many visitors before you, that you are just a little lonely leaving Ireland. Because Ireland is a kind of home for all of us, a home from home for the human heart.

Left: The lush green landscape of Gortin Glen Forest Park, a perfect location for camping holidays.

Commanding spectacular views of Magilligan Strand and the north Antrim coast, Mussenden Temple **(left)** forms part of the remains of Downhill Castle, Co. Derry.
Below: Derry's rugged beauty gives the most serene of sunsets a dazzling backdrop. **Right:** Portstewart, a quiet Victorian resort, is home to sandy beaches and beautiful clifftop scenery, as can be seen in this view from above the town golf club's 2nd green. Not to be outdone, neighbouring Co. Antrim boasts an equally breathtaking coastline – the position of Portrush town's 5th green **(below right)** would distract even the most committed golfer!
Overleaf: fifteen miles south-east of Londonderry lie the Sperrin Mountains, cradling the town of Cranagh and the winding Glenelly River.

The Giant's Causeway **(above left)**, near Bushmills, Co. Antrim, is an extraordinary expanse of polygonal columns formed by the cooling of molten lava. The tallest – the Giant's Organ – stands twelve metres high. A coastal footpath **(above)** offers impressive views of the surrounding headland. **Left:** a glimpse of the lush farmland of north Antrim, near Great Stookan.

The beauty of Co. Antrim's scenery is as spectacular inland as it is on the coast. **Left and below:** Glenariff Forest Park – regarded as the most beautiful of Antrim's nine glens – contains many waterfalls, and its cultivated lower slopes are a rich patchwork of green. South of Glenariff, Antrim's coastline is indented by several picturesque bays; Carnlough **(right)** has a small harbour, while the popular seaside resort of Ballygalley **(below right)** offers magnificent views north up the rugged country of the coast road.

Royal Avenue **(right)** and Donegall Place **(left)** are at the heart of Belfast's pedestrianised shopping quarter. **Below:** the Renaissance-style City Hall serves as a reminder of the city's Edwardian heyday. Standing in Donegall Square, this impressive building was designed by Sir Brumwell Thomas in 1902.
Below left: some five miles east of the city is Stormont – the Parliament buildings. Set in 300 acres of gardens, this English-palladian-style structure forms the administrative centre of the province.

Co. Down boasts the highest mountain range in Ulster. Near the resort of Newcastle, the rugged, moor-covered Mourne Mountains **(right)**, dominated by Slieve Donard, have few surfaced roads, and their footpaths present a challenge to even the most intrepid of visitors. **Above:** the fertile grassland around Dundrum Bay offers a perfect contrast to the mountains beyond.

Separating beautiful Dundalk Bay **(right)** from Carlingford Lough, the scenic Cooley Peninsula **(below left)** is an area that features in the epic legends of ancient Ireland. **Below right:** noted for their high crosses, the spectacular ruins of Monasterboice are to be found a mile west of the main Drogheda to Dundalk road. Founded by St Buithe in the 5th century, this monastery is only a few miles northeast of Mellifont Abbey **(left)**, impressively situated in a secluded valley on the banks of the Mattock River. With its massive square gate tower and 12th-century lavabo, Mellifont was the first Cistercian Abbey to be founded in Ireland.

Situated on the east bank of the Shannon, in Co. Offaly, Clonmacnoise **(above)** is one of Ireland's most important monastic sites. St Ciaran is believed to have founded his monastery here in 548 AD and amongst its remaining treasures are over 400 early Christian grave slabs, some dating from the 8th century. **Above right:** Newgrange, in the Boyne Valley, Co. Meath, is part of the 4,000-year-old Brugh na Boinne burial site, believed to be the oldest man-made structure in the world. **Below right:** the Hill of Slane, also in the Boyne Valley, where St Patrick defied royal decree by kindling the Easter fire, is now occupied by the ruins of a 16th-century church.

Rebuilt in 1929, the General Post Office **(left)**, on Dublin's O'Connell Street, serves as a reminder of the 1916 Insurrection. **Below left:** on the north side of College Green stands the Bank of Ireland. Designed by Sir Edward Lovett Pearce in the early part of the 18th century, its spectacular Ionic 'piazza' is a local landmark. **Right:** the impressive Custom House stands on the banks of the Liffey, its north front featuring a dramatic ox-head frieze. **Below:** seat of the Supreme Court and the High Court of the Republic, the Four Courts on Inns Quay have occupied this site since 1796.

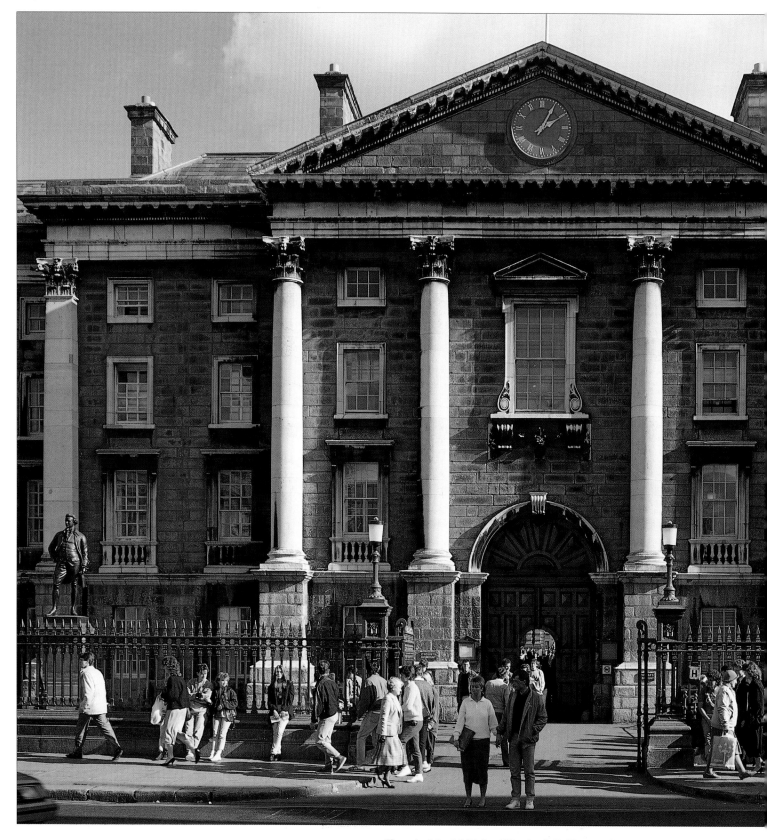

Founded in 1592 by Elizabeth I, Trinity College Dublin has educated some of Ireland's most prominent politicians, poets, philosophers and scientists. With massive reconstruction in the 18th century, almost all of the surviving buildings date from after 1700. Its Palladian-style West Front **(above)** was built between 1752 and 1759. The Quadrangle **(above right)** is dominated by the Campanile, built by Sir Charles Lanyon in 1853. **Right:** St Patrick's Cathedral, on the south side of St Patrick's Park, is the largest church ever built in Ireland, and occupies the site of the pre-Norman parish church. The Great Tower was built by Archbishop Minot in 1381.

Left: O'Connell Street – the bustling heart of the city.
Right: the statue of Molly Malone, in Grafton Street. **Below:** the St Stephen's Green shopping centre. Situated on the north-west corner of the green, this light, airy and spacious building complements the venerable splendour of Dublin's Georgian architecture.

Razed by Cromwell's forces in 1650, the ruins of the castle atop the forbidding Rock of Dunamase **(right)** contrast with the peaceful countryside **(above)** near Timahoe, Co. Laois. **Left:** Blackstairs Mountains scenery near Ballymurphy, Co. Carlow.

Above: the splendid view towards Lough Tay from the vantage point of Sally Gap. Although not as dramatic, the local Wicklow countryside – near the source of the Inchavore River **(right)**, and surrounding Lough Dan **(top right)** – is no less beautiful.

Left: the falls of the Glenmacnass River, near Laragh, Co. Wicklow. To the north-east rises the 1,600-foot mass of Great Sugar Loaf **(below)**, near the resort town of Greystones. Complementing the region's natural beauty is the splendour of Powerscourt, the shell of an 18th-century mansion destroyed by fire in 1974. The surrounding landscaped gardens are justly famous.

The superb coastline of Co. Wexford. **Above left:** Hook Head lighthouse, which stands at the entrance to Waterford Harbour, is surrounded by coral-encrusted limestone cliffs. **Left:** the dramatic headland near the town of Fethard; this area saw the first invading force of the Anglo-Normans in 1169. **Above:** Kilmore Quay, a seaside village at the eastern end of Ballyteige Bay. Noted for its lobsters and deep-sea fishing, it is also the point of departure for the nearby Saltee Islands, some four miles distant.

Set in magnificent grounds, Johnstown Castle **(above)**, in Co. Wexford is a 19th-century Gothic mansion, now state-owned and used as an agricultural college. Approximately fifteen miles west of Johnstown is the John F. Kennedy Memorial Park **(right),** situated near the Kennedy family ancestral home at Dunganstown. This beautiful arboretum contains thousands of trees donated from all around the world. **Overleaf:** Inistioge, a picturesque village on the banks of the River Nore.

At Ardmore, Co. Waterford, the round tower **(left)** dominates the 5th-century remains of St Declan's settlements. Erected in the 12th century, the ninety-six-foot tower is one of the most complete of its kind in Ireland. **Right:** the Monavullagh Mountains form a magnificent backdrop to Dungarvan's fine harbour **(overleaf).** Further north, the Comeragh range **(below)** rises to a height of almost 2,600 feet.

The town of Cashel, Co. Tipperary, is overshadowed by the famous Rock of Cashel **(right)**, which from the 4th to the 12th century was a stronghold of the kings of Munster. After being visited by St Patrick who preached the doctrine of the Trinity there in the 5th century, it acquired a much greater significance, passing into Church ownership in the 12th century. The oldest surviving structure is the eighty-five-foot round tower.

Once an important pass between the plains of Tipperary and Limerick, the remote Glen of Aherlow **(left)** is situated between the Galtee Mountains and Slievenamuck Hills. It was the site of many battles between the feuding O'Briens and Fitzpatricks. **Below:** the view near Portroe, across the twenty-five-mile-long Lough Derg to Clare, Galway and Tipperary. **Right:** straddling the border between Tipperary and Wexford, the Knockmealdown Mountains afford stunning views of the Galtee, Comeragh and Kilworth ranges. **Below right:** the view across to Moneygall, Co. Offaly, from Co. Tipperary.

The view along the River Lee at Sullivan's Quay **(above)**, affords a charming view of St Finbarr's Cathedral. Designed in the 19th century by William Burgess, this French-gothic-style building occupies the site of the original monastery, founded in the 6th-7th century.
Below: Cork city's Grand Parade, at its junction with Oliver Plunkett Street which forms part of Cork's busy centre.
Right: the view along Parnell Place reveals some of the colour and charm of this welcoming city.

50

The brightly painted pub and store fronts in Cork's towns and villages reflect the warmth of the welcome to be found within.

Dromberg Stone Circle **(left)** near Glandore, Co. Cork, is an important archaeological site whose purpose is subject to much conjecture. **Below:** Blarney Castle, the 15th-century stronghold that withstood the attack of Cromwell's men. The famous Blarney Stone **(right)** is said to bestow the gift of eloquence upon anyone who kisses it – no mean feat as it still forms part of the battlements of the castle!

THERE IS NO CHARGE FOR
KISSING THE BLARNEY STONE
REMOVE ALL LOOSE VALUABLES
BEFORE DOING SO

Co. Cork is blessed with a wealth of spectacular coastal scenery. The golden sands of Barley Cove **(left)**, near Crookhaven, contrast with the dramatic, near-vertical cliffs of neighbouring Mizen Head **(above)**, whose lighthouse has been witness to countless maritime disasters.

The popular image of Ireland as a gently undulating pastoral landscape is only partly true. In Cork the majestic Caha Mountains **(left)** stretch the length of the Beara Peninsula, joining the Slieve Miskish **(below and below right),** whose rocky fingers dip into the cold waters of the Atlantic. **Right:** afternoon sun on the Shehy Mountains. **Overleaf:** the Healy Pass links Counties Cork and Kerry, affording some of the finest views in Ireland.

Situated amid the Kerry Hills at the point where the Roughty River meets the Kenmare River, picturesque Kenmare **(above)** is a small market town and popular angling resort founded by Sir William Petty in 1670. Like nearby Parknasilla **(right),** it serves as an ideal starting point for tours of the Ring of Kerry and the rugged Macgillycuddy's Reeks.

The Ring of Kerry – the name given to the 109-mile circuit of the Iveragh Peninsula – features some of the most beautiful scenery in Ireland. The route passes through the village of Sneem **(these pages),** which offers its own attractions.
Overleaf: one of the beautiful Loughs in the Ring of Kerry.

Both beautiful and historically important, Derrynane was for centuries home to the O'Connells, one of Ireland's most celebrated political families. The harbour **(left)** and bay **(below)** are typical of the scenery to be found in this area, and the view across to Scariff Island **(right)** is breathtaking. **Overleaf:** Caherdaniel, the village that takes its name from the stone fort half a mile west.

The spectacular Gap of Dunloe **(left)** separates the Tomies and Purple Mountains from Macgillycuddy's Reeks. As well as containing the highest peaks in Ireland – several exceeding 3,000 feet – the Reeks cradle some beautiful lakes. Lough Acoose **(right)** and Lough Leane **(below)**, near Killarney, are but two examples. **Overleaf:** Carrantuohill – at 3,414 feet, this is the highest peak in Macgillycuddy's Reeks.

Rich in history and magnificent scenery, the Dingle Peninsula is small enough to be toured in a day, but offers sights that should be enjoyed at leisure. **Right:** the spectacular headland at Doon Point. **Left:** Connor Pass. **Below:** the prehistoric remains of the circular stone fort of Cahernamactirea, not far from the beautiful strand at Coumeenoole **(below right).**

The gentle landscape of the Corra valley **(above),** Co. Clare, and near Cortaheera **(right and above right). Overleaf:** Ennistymon, on the River Cullenagh, noted for its excellent fishing.

Reaching a height of 700 feet, the bastion-like Cliffs of Moher rise sheer from the foaming waters of the Atlantic. Extending for some five miles, they are crowned at their north-eastern end by O'Brien's Tower, constructed in 1835 to allow visitors to experience the view in safety.

Bare limestone terraces that shelter
rare Alpine flora, potholes,
underground caverns and disappearing
streams characterise the Burren's 50
square miles. The hand of prehistoric
man can be glimpsed here, too, in the
form of numerous stone forts and
dolmens.

Sitting at the head of Kinvarra Bay, an inlet of the larger Galway Bay, the town of Kinvarra thrived as an exporter of local grain in the 19th century, but has since lost more than half of its population. Today, this sleepy village draws much of its livelihood from the sea.

Left: the Twelve Bens seen across the serene waters of Bertraghboy Bay, near Roundstone. **Right:** sunset over Clifden Bay, and **(below)** Slyne Head, on the western tip of the Ballyconneelly Peninsula.

The rugged, unspoilt beauty of Connemara **(above)** is apparent in every view, but particularly so around its coastline. The view across Clifden Bay **(above left)** reveals the stark beauty of the Twelve Bens. West of Clifden Bay lies Kingstown Bay **(left and overleaf).**

Built in the 19th century by a wealthy Liverpool merchant, Kylemore Abbey stands on the northern shore of Pollacappul Lough. Originally a palatial mansion, it now serves as a boarding school and convent run by Benedictine nuns. Access to the Abbey is via the Pass of Kylemore, widely considered to be the most beautiful place in Connemara.

Leenane **(left),** in Co. Galway, sits at the south-east corner of Killary Harbour. The fjord-like harbour **(below and right)** is the drowned lower valley of the Erriff River and once served as a British naval base. Leenane itself is a popular fishing and shooting resort, and is the perfect base from which to explore the surrounding mountains and the rest of Connemara.

Ashford Castle **(left and below left),** in Co. Mayo, was once the home of the Guinness family and is now a hotel. Constructed by J.H. Fuller in 1870 around an earlier mansion and tower house, the castle lies about a mile north of the village of Cong. Cong Abbey **(right and below right)** was founded by King Turloch Mór O'Connor, early in the 12th century. His son Rory, the last king of Ireland, retired to the monastery in 1183 and died there in 1198. The delicate, Gothic details in the doorways **(right)** are a fine example of Irish medieval stone carving. The only original surviving part of the cloisters **(below right)** is the first arch and its coupled columns. **Below:** the lush, tranquil landscape of Co. Mayo.

Of special significance to all Irishmen, Croagh Patrick **(these pages)**, Co. Mayo, is the mountain on which the patron saint is reputed to have spent forty days and nights in prayer and fasting. His statue **(above)** stands at the foot of the mountain, overlooking Clew Bay. **Overleaf:** sunset silhouettes the 2,646-foot bulk of Nephin, across the cold waters of Lough Conn.

Awe-inspiring Benbulben, the great
table-topped mountain in Co. Sligo's
Dartry Mountains, dominates the
surrounding landscape. The incised
western edge plunges some 1,500 feet
to the flat coastal plains below.

Left: Carrick-on-Shannon, the county
town of Leitrim. Situated on the banks
of the Shannon, the town is famed for
its fine fishing. **Above:** beautiful
Glencar Lough, whose waters are
shared by both Sligo and Leitrim.
Overleaf: the church at Drumcliff,
looking towards Glencar Lough.

Lough Swilly **(left and overleaf),** in Co. Donegal, extends for over twenty-five miles between the Inishowen Peninsula and the narrower Fanad Peninsula to the west. The surrounding scenery **(right and below right)** is characteristic of Donegal, with sandy beaches and rocky coves.
Below: the landscape around the Grianan of Aileach, the ancient seat of the kings of Ulster, which was inhabited from the Stone Age up until the 12th century. **Last page:** a magnificent sunset over Trawbreaga Bay, on the Inishowen Peninsula.